First Facts®

FACT FILES

CONTINENTS

What You Need to Know

by JILL SHERMAN

raintree

a Capstone company — publishers for children

Edited by Mandy Robbins
Designed by Jenny Bergstrom
Picture research by Kelly Garvin
Production by Laura Manthe
Originated by Capstone Global Library Limited
Printed and bound in China.

ISBN 978-1-4747-4890-2
21 20 19 18 17
10 9 8 7 6 5 4 3 2 1

British Library Cataloguing in Publication Data
A full catalogue record for this book is available from the British Library.

Acknowledgements
We would like to thank the following for permission to reproduce photographs: Shutterstock: Adwo, 15, (bottom left), Andrzej Kubik, 15 (middle right), Arthur Balitskiy, 5, Bardocz Peter, cover (top left, bottom right), 1, Bildagentur Zoonar GmBbH, cover (top right, bl), Bill Chariya, 19 (inset), Daniel Prudek, 8, Designua, 3, EcoPrint, 7, Filipe Frazao, 15 (tl) (br), InnervisionArt, 9, Kristian Bell, 16, LUMOimages, 12, Norimoto, 20, Olga Danylenko, 21, Phanom Nuangchomphoo, 13, pisaphotography, 22, S.Borisov, 11-12, szefei, 24, Tookrub, 17, Vaclav Volrab, 6, Vadim Petrakov, 15 (tr), Wojciech Dziadosz, 18-19

Design Elements:
Shutterstock/Mikko Lemola

We would like to thank Paige Roth for her invaluable help in the preparation of this book.

Contents

Arctic Ocean

NORTH
AMERICA

Atlantic
Ocean

Pacific
Ocean

AFRICA

SOUTH
AMERICA

A giant land mass

Land and water cover Earth. Look at a world map. You can count seven large land masses. They are **continents**. Each is entirely or mostly surrounded by water.

Long ago, all of Earth's land was joined. Scientists call this single land mass Pangaea. Pangaea began to drift apart about 200 million years ago. It broke into today's seven continents.

continent – one of Earth's seven large land masses

DRIFTING
CONTINENTS

225

MILLION YEARS AGO

150

MILLION YEARS AGO

65

MILLION YEARS AGO

Present

Africa

Africa is home to the Sahara, the world's largest **desert**. It also has the longest river, the Nile. Many impressive wild animals live in Africa. They include lions, giraffes and elephants. Most scientists agree the first humans lived in Africa too.

FACT

Africa is a huge **plateau**. Most of its land is high above sea level. Then it drops off sharply at the coast.

desert – a dry area with little rain
plateau – an area of high, flat land

SIZE

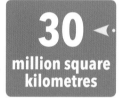

30

million square kilometres

(11.6 million square miles)

NUMBER OF COUNTRIES

54

POPULATION

more than

1

billion

Asia

Asia is Earth's largest continent. More people live there than in any other continent. Asia is a land of extremes. To the north lies the frozen Arctic Ocean. In the south there are *tropical* jungles. Asia also has thick forests, large deserts and long rivers.

tropical – having to do with hot and wet areas near the equator

8

SIZE

44.5
million square
kilometres

(17.2 million
square miles)

NUMBER OF
COUNTRIES

50

POPULATION

4.5
billion

Europe

Europe is west of Asia. It is the second smallest continent. But it has a large **population**. Other continents have wide-open spaces. People occupy most of Europe.

Europe and Asia are part of the same land mass. Some scientists consider them one continent called Eurasia.

population – a group of people, animals or plants living in a certain place

POPULATION DENSITY

Check out the average number of people living in one square kilometre on each continent.

SIZE

10.4

million square kilometres

(4 million square miles)

NUMBER OF COUNTRIES

49

POPULATION

724
million

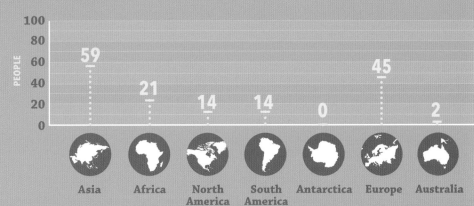

	Asia	Africa	North America	South America	Antarctica	Europe	Australia
PEOPLE	59	21	14	14	0	45	2

North America

North America lies across the Atlantic Ocean from Europe. It has every type of land and **climate**. There are mountains, deserts, forests and swamps. People in northern areas live in very cold temperatures. Those in southern countries have tropical weather.

climate – average weather of a place throughout the year

NORTH AMERICA

SIZE

24.1
million square kilometres

(9.3 million square miles)

NUMBER OF COUNTRIES

23

POPULATION

more than
572
million

13

South America

South America has many natural wonders. The Amazon **rainforest** is the world's largest rainforest. The Amazon River carries 15 to 20 per cent of Earth's fresh water to the ocean. Angel Falls in Venezuela is the world's highest waterfall. The Andes are the longest mountain range. The Atacama Desert is one of the hottest, driest places on Earth.

rainforest – a thick forest where rain falls almost every day

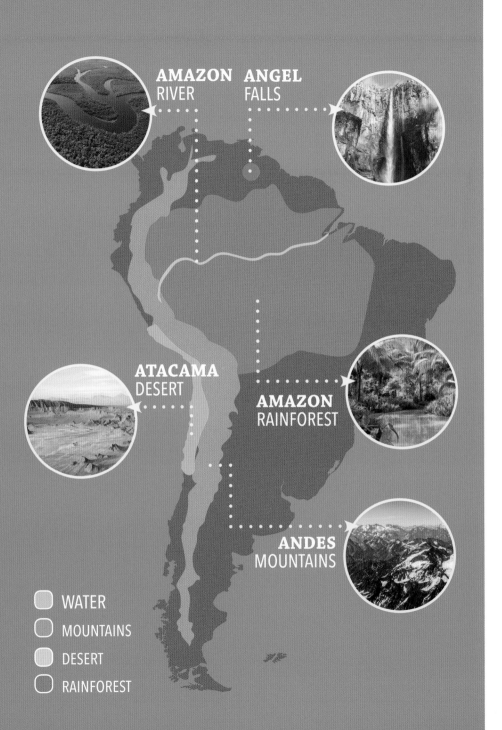

AMAZON RIVER

ANGEL FALLS

ATACAMA DESERT

AMAZON RAINFOREST

ANDES MOUNTAINS

WATER

MOUNTAINS

DESERT

RAINFOREST

SOUTH AMERICA

SIZE

17.6
million square kilometres

(6.8 million square miles)

NUMBER OF COUNTRIES

12

POPULATION

more than **418** million

15

Australia

Australia is the largest island in the world. But it is the smallest continent. Australia is the only continent that is also one country. There are mountains and cities in the east. Western Australia is home to dry deserts and grasslands. Few people live in the west.

FACT

Australia is known to have many poisonous animals. It has more deadly snakes than any other country.

AT A GLANCE:
AUSTRALIA

SIZE

7.5 ◄
million square kilometres

(2.9 million
square miles)

NUMBER OF COUNTRIES

•••► **1**

POPULATION

more than

24 ◄••
million

Antarctica

Antarctica is the coldest, windiest place on Earth. An ice sheet covers the land. A few mountains rise above the ice. Without its ice, Antarctica would look much smaller.

People visit Antarctica, but no one makes it their home. Many scientists study Antarctica. It has more than 40 research stations.

ANTARCTICA

Antarctica's ice is 4.8 kilometres (3 miles) thick in some places.

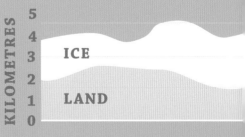

KILOMETRES
5
4
3 ICE
2
1 LAND
0

ANTARCTICA ICE SHEET AREA

LAND

ICE

Maps of Antarctica include its ice sheet. The land beneath is much smaller than what is shown on a map.

4.8 KILOMETRES THICK

SIZE

14 ◄

million square kilometres

(5.4 million square miles)

NUMBER OF COUNTRIES

··► **0**

POPULATION

0 ◄··

VISITORS

1,000 in winter

4,500 in summer

Oceania

Some places are not part of any continent. About 30,000 islands dot the Pacific Ocean. They are part of an area called Oceania.

Some large islands are countries. Papua New Guinea and New Zealand are Pacific island nations. Other islands are tiny. They barely rise above the ocean's surface.

FACT
Some people consider Australia part of Oceania. Others don't because Australia is its own continent.

AT A GLANCE:
OCEANIA

more than
776,000
square kilometres

(300,000
square miles)

**NUMBER OF
COUNTRIES**

13

POPULATION

20
million

Glossary

climate average weather of a place throughout the year

continent one of Earth's seven large land masses

desert a dry area with little rain

plateau an area of high, flat land

population a group of people, animals, or plants living in a certain place

rainforest a thick forest where rain falls almost every day

tropical having to do with the hot and wet areas near the equator

Read more

Continents (Fact Cat: Geography), Izzi Howell (Wayland, 2016)

Continents (Infographics), Harriet Bundle (Book Life, 2017)

Factivity Atlas: Explore the Wonders of Your World, Anita Ganeri (Parragon, 2016)

Websites

www.dkfindout.com/uk/earth/continents/

Visit this interactive website to find information about the seven continents.

www.bbc.co.uk/education/topics/z3fycdm

This BBC website has video clips about interesting places in different continents.

mrnussbaum.com/continents/

This website has an interactive world map: click on each continent to find out more about it.

Critical thinking questions

1. Reread pages 10 through 13. How are Europe and North America alike? How are they different?

2. Which of the continents would you most like to visit? Why?

3. Which continent is most different from the others? How is it different?

Index